This Book Belongs To: ....

....

....

....

COLOR TEST PAGE

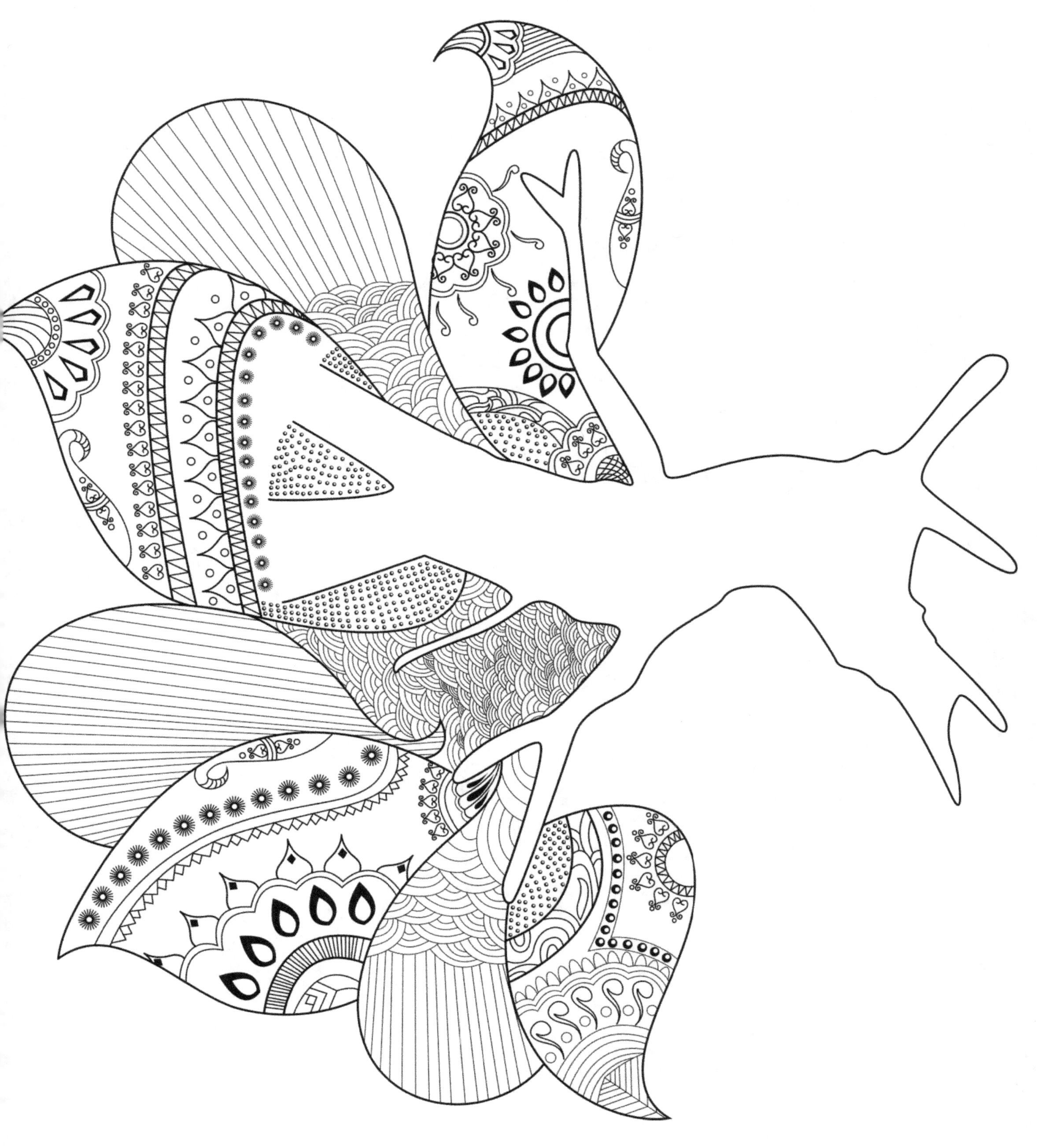

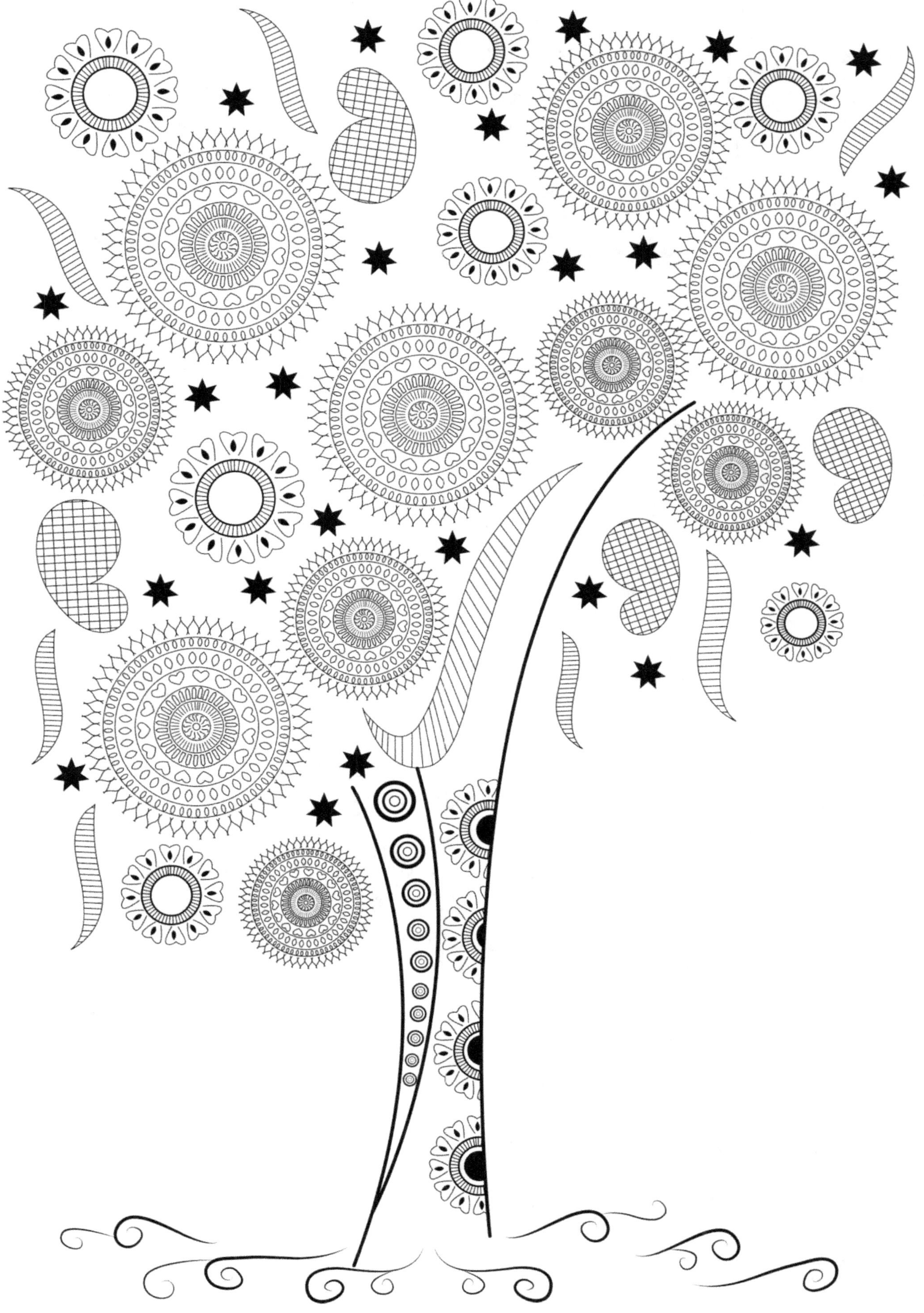

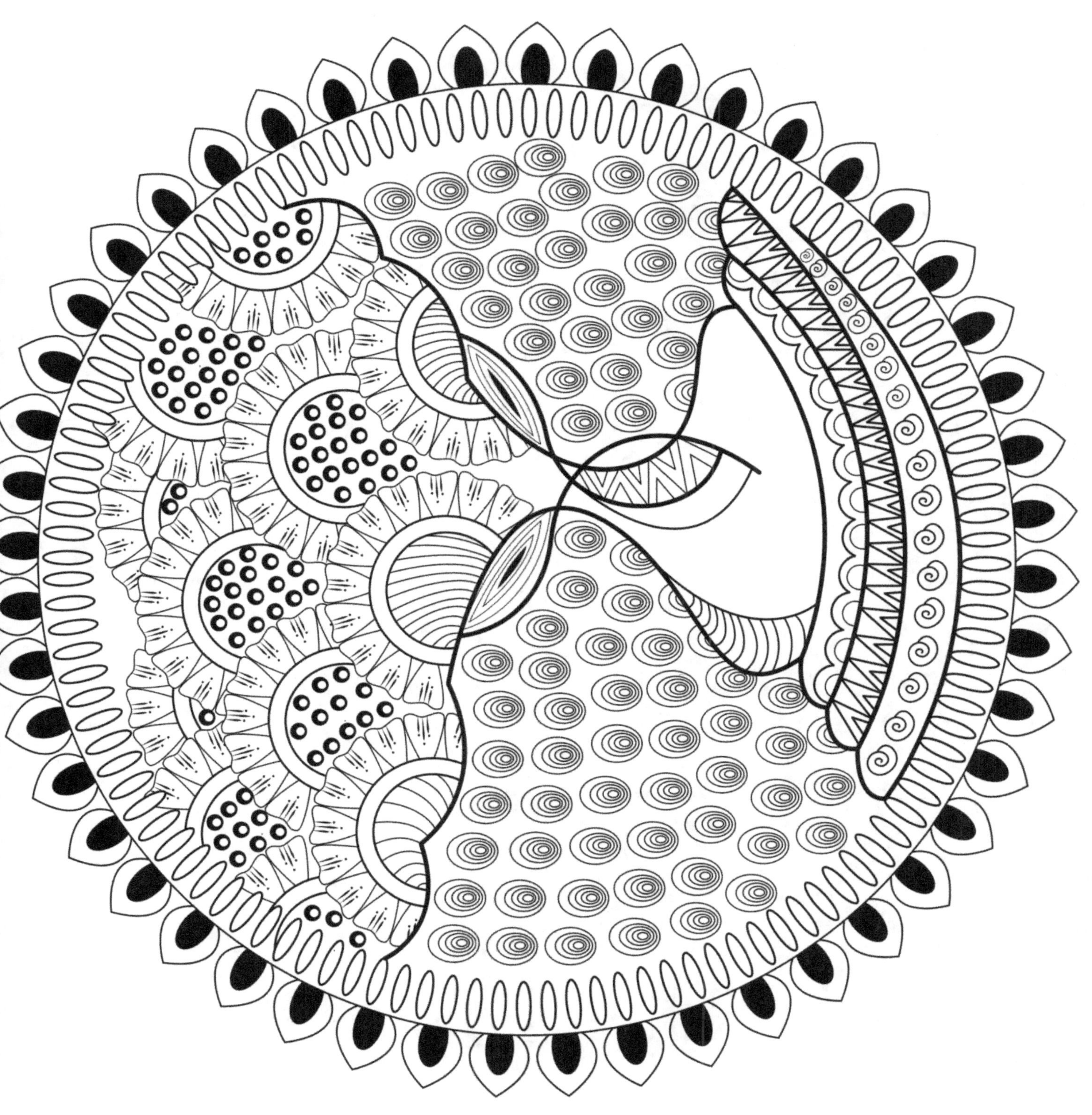

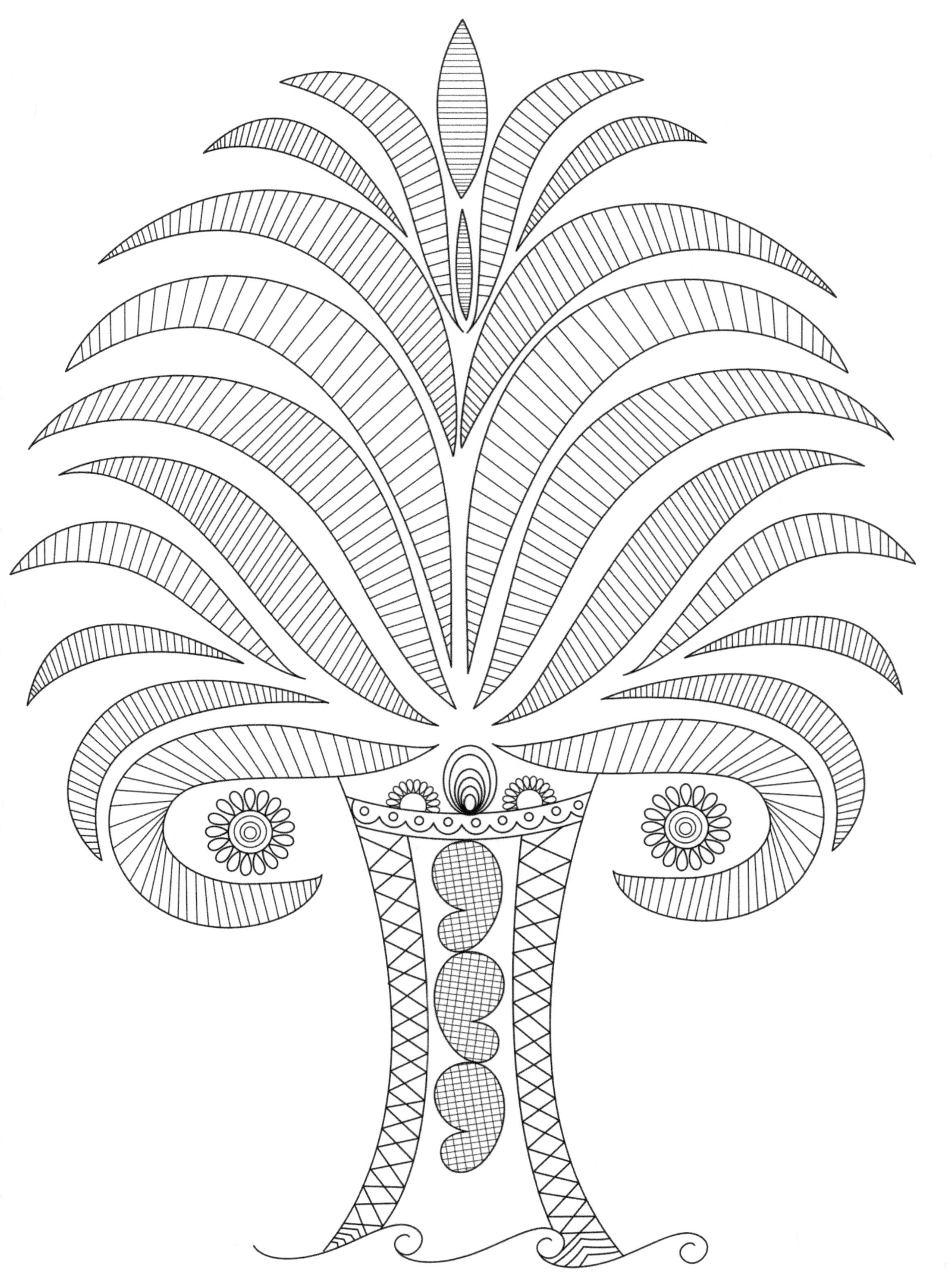

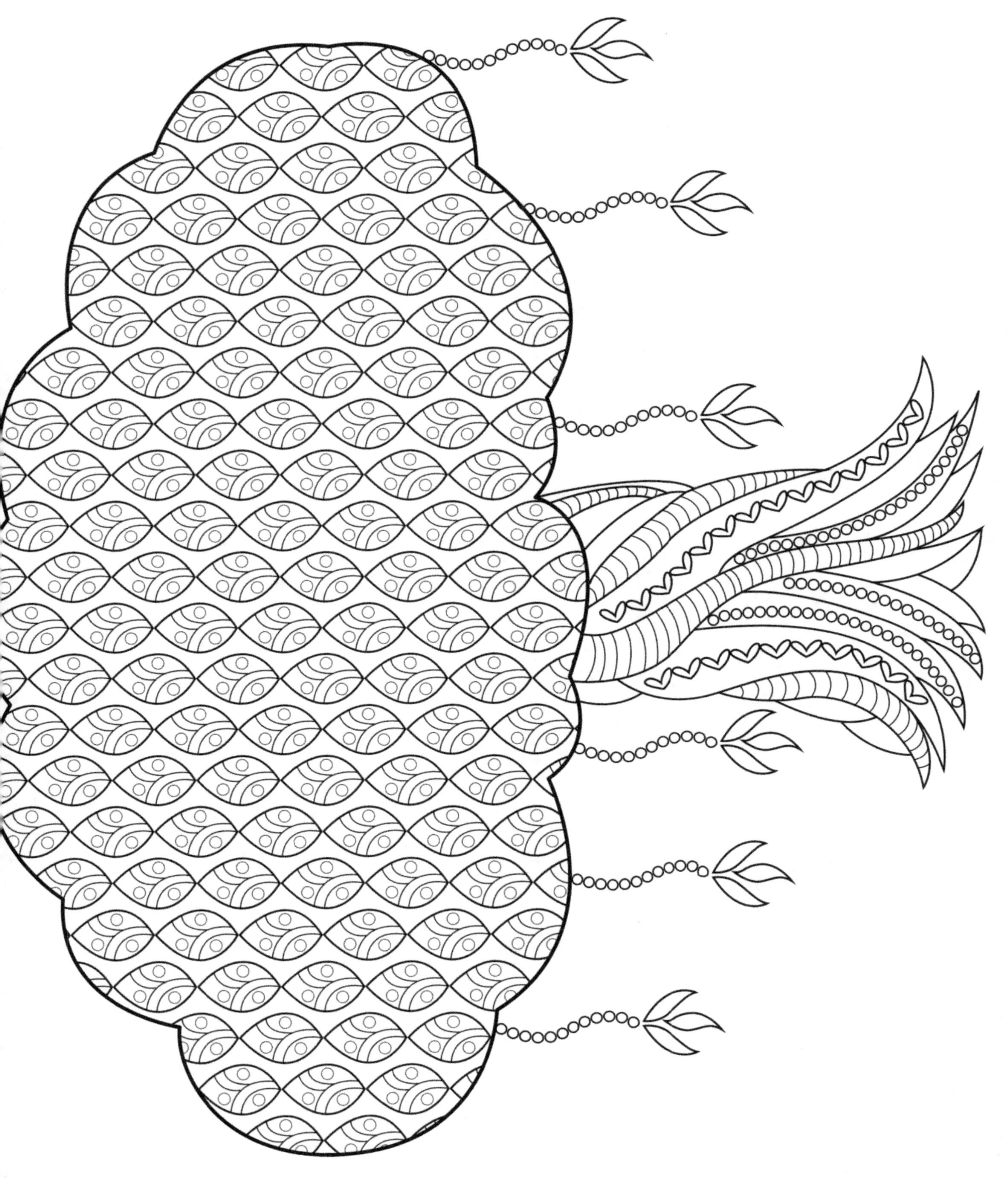

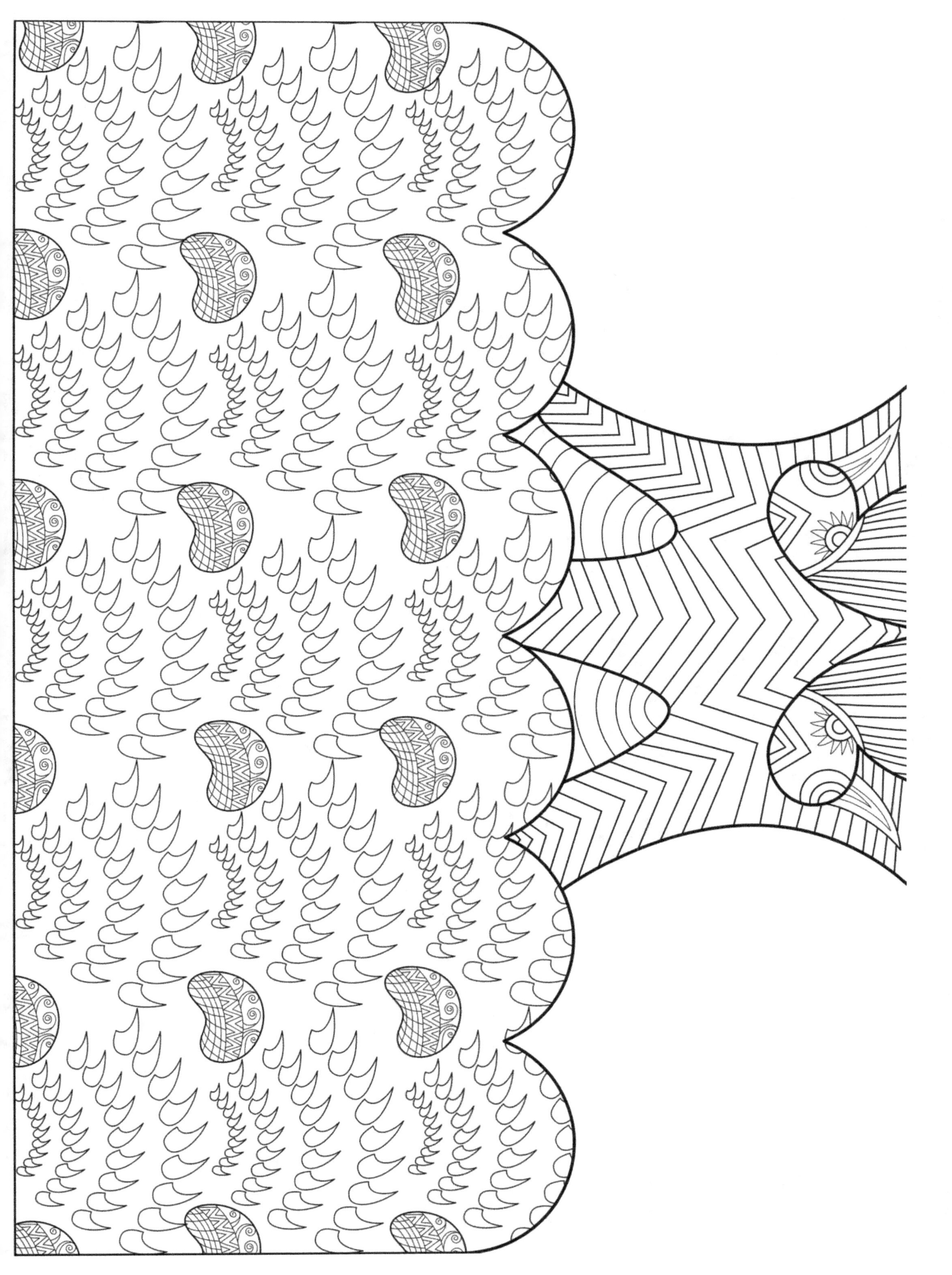